ISBN:
Hardback 978-1-922593-00-9
Digital 978-1-922593-01-6

BB & Tills Publishing
Copyright © Amy Marley 2021. All rights reserved.

For Billie, Matilda, Amelia, Lucien, Daniel, Ben, Emma, Winter
and humans of all ages living with allergies

Special thanks to Rosee Maxwell, Letizia Petti
and the countless others around the world who have
kindly gifted their time, support and feedback.

**Proceeds donated to
Allergy Support Hub and Allergy Life Australia**

This book contains stock photography, royalty free images
and the author's personal photographs.

Special thanks to all the photographers!

©Pete the Peanut was designed by Amy Marley

Preface

Pete The Peanut is an introductory resource for kids of all ages to read with their parents, families, teachers, carers, specialists, aunts, uncles and whoever will read it with them!

Before reading this resource with a child, it is recommended you review the photos and text.

<u>**Some photos used may be disturbing**</u>

Each of us are at different stages of the allergy journey and nobody processes the journey in exactly the same way.

You may feel certain parts are not yet appropriate. No right, no wrong—only what suits you and your family.

This resource doesn't have to be read all at once. Dip in and out of the information as needed.

As a parent new to the allergy game, I found it challenging managing risks day to day. Reactions can be rare, so it isn't always easy to comprehend what is involved until the moment is lived.

My daughter was only one when we learned she was prone to anaphylactic reactions to peanuts, tree nuts and eggs.

By the time she was 3 and off to kindergarten, she was still learning what nuts and eggs were and could barely say the word "anaphylaxis."

My intention then, and now, is to empower her with enough information so she can self-advocate in a world filled with distractions.

The use of photos vs illustrations ensures there is no room for "make-believe".

Allergies are **REAL**. Reactions are **REAL**.

While we can't allergy proof the world, using our voices and sharing information is a powerful way to expand the awareness of allergies.

Share your story often. It needs to be heard.

Please reach out to talk to someone if you are feeling excess fear or anxiety while managing allergies. There are brilliant psychologists, counsellors and support groups who specialise in allergies.

A list of resources is available at https://amymarley.com/resources/

THIS BOOK SHOULD NOT BE RELIED
UPON AS AN ALTERNATIVE TO DOCTOR'S ADVICE

Each allergy case is different.

Please see your doctor to confirm individual requirements.

Pete the Peanut

An Introductory Resource to Allergens, Allergies & Anaphylaxis

by Amy Marley

This is Pete. Pete's a peanut.

Say hi, Pete.

This is Pete in his shell,

Pete in his second skin

and Pete — ***naked!***

This is Pete halved

and Pete — *chopped!*

Pete grew in the ground.

Even though nut appears in his name,

Pete is a ***legume***, not a ***nut***.

Pete can trigger allergic reactions in people who have allergies.

Let's find out more about Pete and allergies.

Like learning where I hang out?!

Yep! Exactly, Pete.

Pete likes to hang out with other peanuts in products like

cereals

muesli bars

oils

and chocolates.

I can also be an ingredient in food like...
satay
curry
salad
stir fry
dip
sauces and marinades.

soaps and lotions

medicine and makeup.

Arachis/arachis hypogea is how it may appear on these labels

Pete can leave traces in places.

Sorry!
I don't mean to
leave a mess.

Like
food factories

in weigh-n-pay

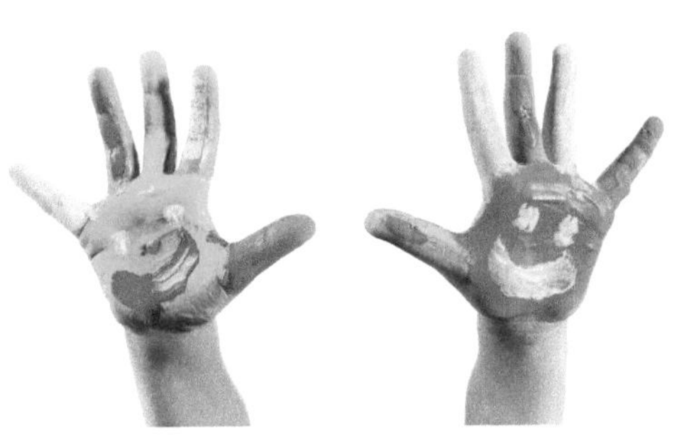

on hands and lips

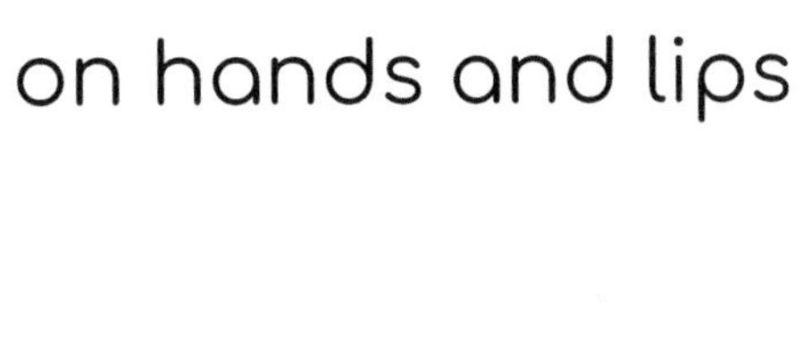

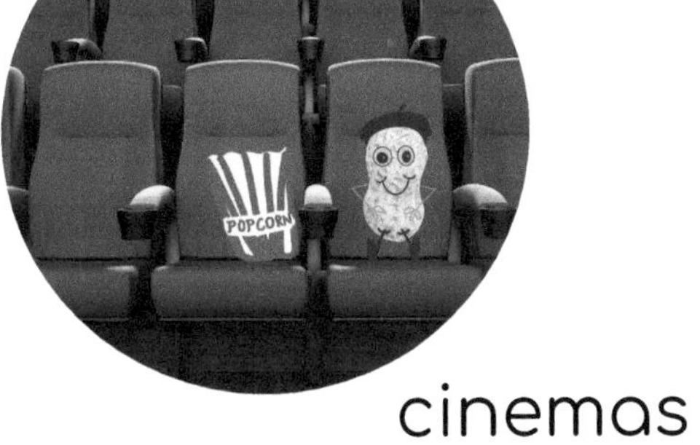

cinemas

restaurants

trains, planes and buses.

And, sometimes I can show up on...
chopping boards
water bottles
forks, knives, spoons
dishes, pots and pans.

Pete can also be
at parties,
play centres and
playgrounds.

To keep everyone safe, whether they have allergies or not ...

BEFORE
eating or sharing food

using drink bottles

putting hands
in or near mouths

or
kissing lips...

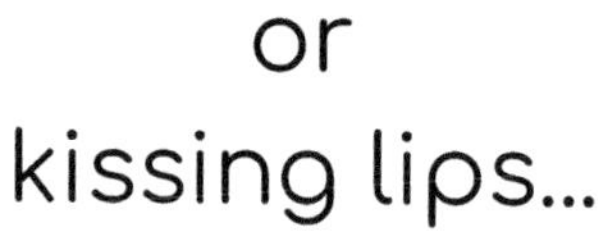

Ewww...
Kissing!!

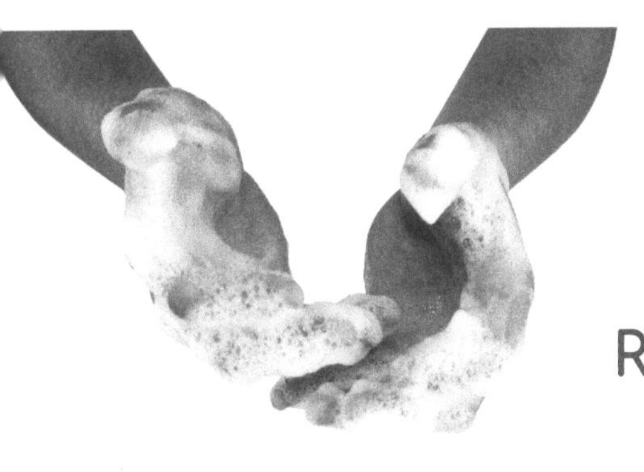

Remember!

Wash your hands, mouth, lips and dishes.

Read ingredient lists and allergy warnings on all food packaging.

Ingredients
Corn (60%), sugar, peanuts
salt, barley malt extract,
vitamin B6, riboflavin, Folate),
Contains gluten, peanuts.
May contain wheat, tree
INGREDIENTS: Stone ground white corn, sunflower oil or corn oil, red beet, flaxseed, black sesame seeds, ground paprika, chia seeds, onion, sea salt.
ALLERGY INFORMATION: Made in a facility that uses dairy, soy, sesame seeds and flaxseed.
Made in a peanut free facility.

Use your voice to check if you are unsure.

Pete can be sneaky.

That's true.
I'm really good
at playing
hide and seek!

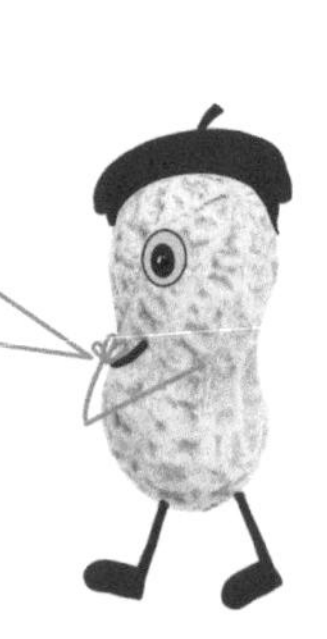

Let's see what can happen when someone allergic to Pete finds him by accident.

Pete can do unexpected things to people with allergies, like making

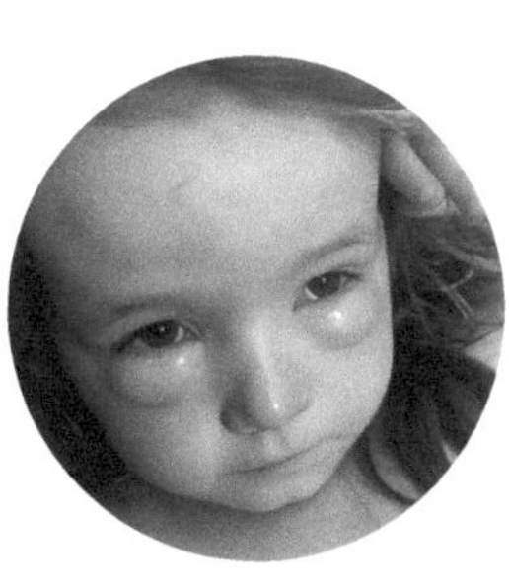

faces swell and puff

skin itch

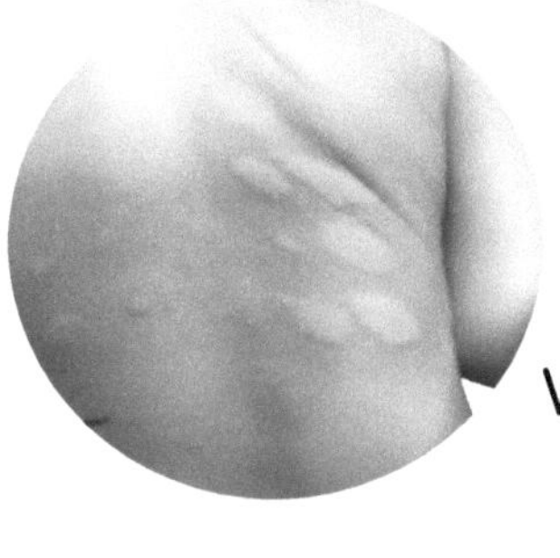

welts or hives appear

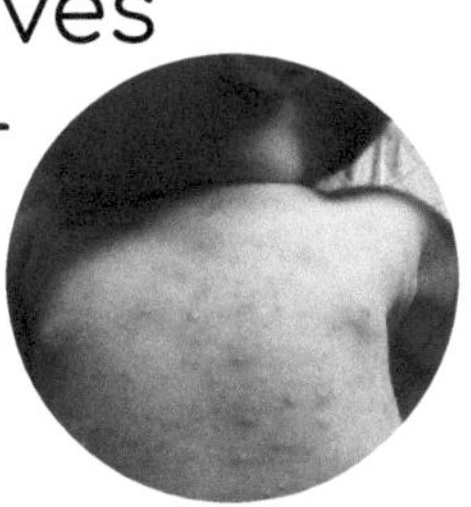

and tummies vomit.

Signs Pete may be causing
a severe allergic reaction are...

trouble breathing

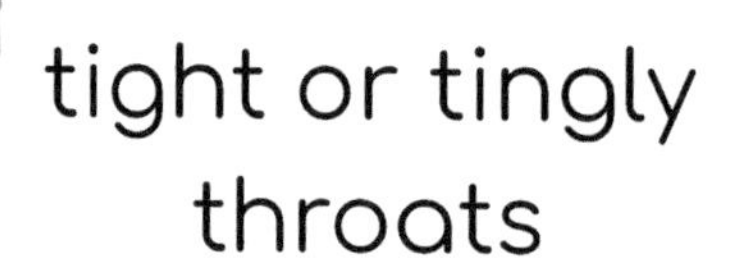

tight or tingly
throats

swelling tongues

coughing or wheezing

becoming pale or floppy

I don't mean to do this!!

feeling dizzy or collapsing.

If you, a friend or a family member
have **ANY** of these symptoms,
even for the first time,
tell an adult.

An adult is almost always around
but if not,
YOU can still help.

If a person is
having trouble breathing
has swelling of the tongue
tightness in the throat
wheezing, is persistently coughing
dizzy, pale, floppy or
has collapsed
consider it to be
Anaphylaxis in action

Make sure the person is
sitting or lying flat

Do not let them stand or walk

Remember anaphylaxis is life threatening

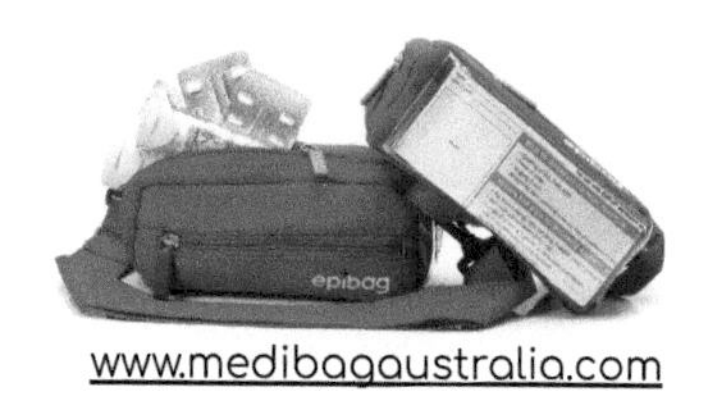

www.medibagaustralia.com

Action plans,

medications

and adrenaline pens

are kept at schools,

daycares,

in first aid kits

or carried by those

who have allergic and

anaphylactic reactions.

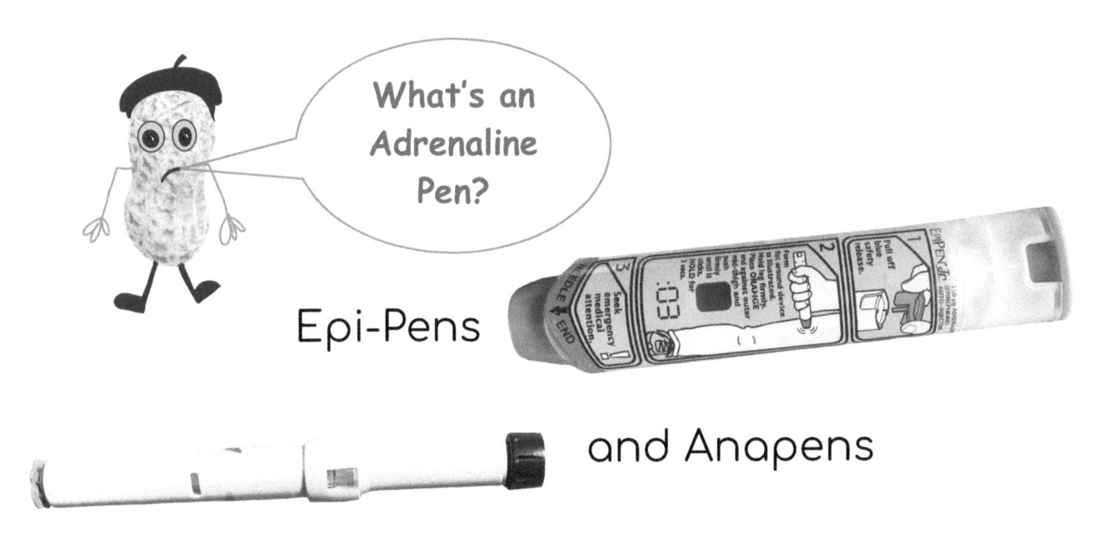
What's an Adrenaline Pen?

Epi-Pens

and Anapens

are two types of adrenaline pens that can be used during an anaphylactic reaction to help stop it.

No Adrenaline Pen?
Stay calm,
Make sure the person is
sitting or lying flat
monitor
and call **000***
for an ambulance.

* **000** (Australia) **111** (NZ), **112** (mobile/International Standard Emergency Number), **911** (US/CAN), **999** (UK)

How to use an Epi-Pen

Grip the Epi-Pen
with one hand

It's ok to use
through pants and jeans
Just keep away
from pockets and seams

Blue to the sky
Orange to the outer-mid-thigh

Remove the blue cap

Push hard to hear the click
This releases the needle prick

Hold, and count 1 2 3
To set the adrenaline free
Remove the Epi-Pen gently

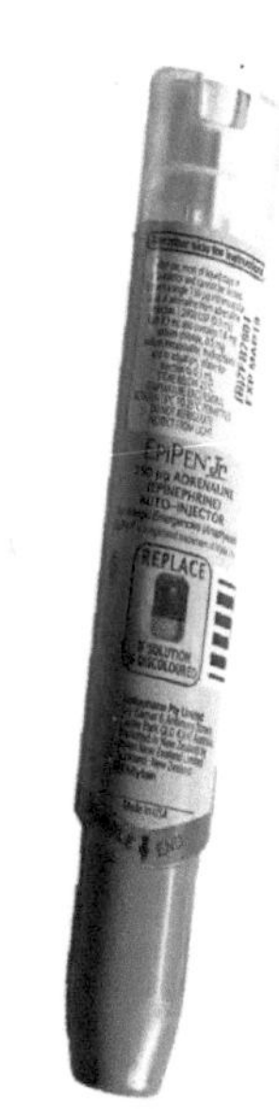

After administered, the orange end of the epi-pen will cover the needle prick

How to use an Anapen

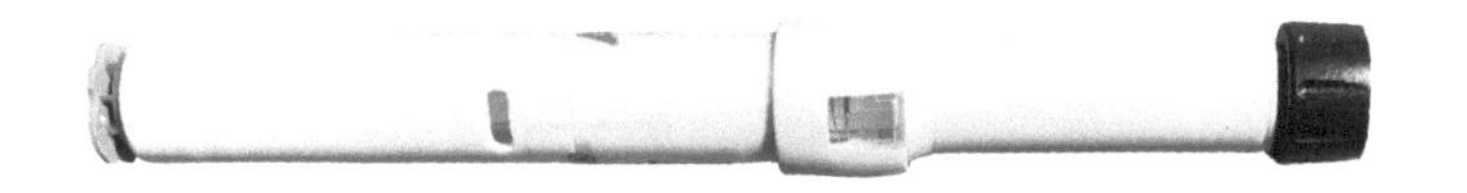

Pull off the **black** needle shield
and grey safety cap from the red button

It's ok to use
through pants and jeans
Just keep away
from pockets and seams

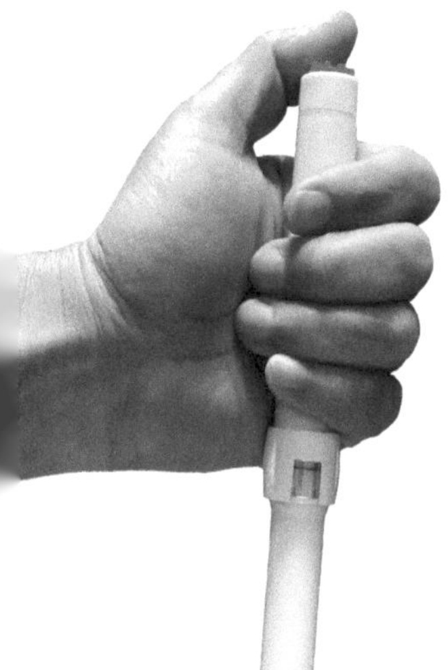

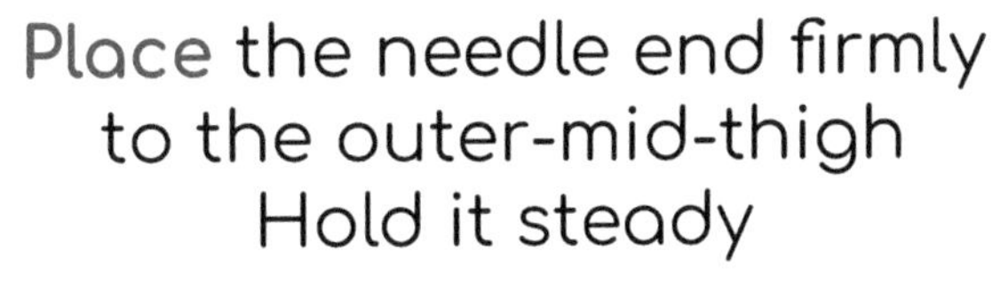

Place the needle end firmly
to the outer-mid-thigh
Hold it steady

Press the red button
to release the needle prick

Hold, and count to 10
To set the adrenaline free
Remove the Anapen gently

Careful not to touch the exposed needle.
When possible, place the black needle shield over the needle.

Now use the phone
Don't leave the person alone

Call **000***
Ask for an ambulance
It's an emergency!

Follow the operator's instructions
until the ambulance arrives

While waiting,
a second adrenaline pen
can be used
if signs don't improve

Then it's off to hospital
for monitoring
and more medical care

* **000** (Australia) **111** (NZ), **112** (mobile/International Standard Emergency Number), **911** (US/CAN), **999** (UK)

After hospital,
no matter how many reactions
someone has had,

finding out as much
information
as possible,

keeps everyone having fun
while staying aware.

Allergists check
if I caused a reaction,
assess the risks and
suggest treatments.

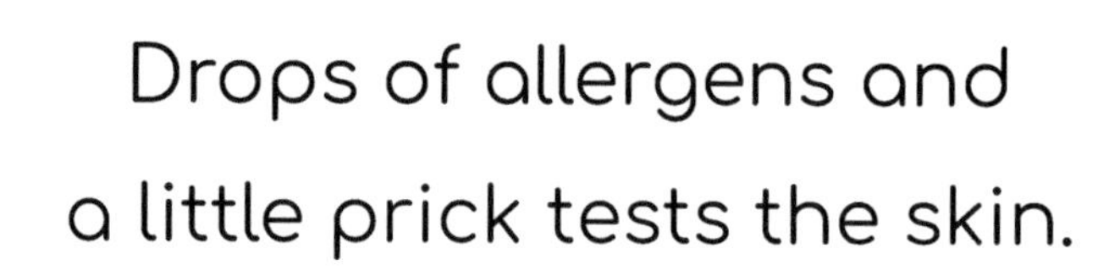

Drops of allergens and
a little prick tests the skin.

Blood tests
measure antibodies
called **IgE** —
short for ***Immunoglobulin E.***

As bodies grow and change,
regular visits with allergists help to
safely test, tweak treatments

and may even show
an allergy
has been outgrown.

Extra Bits to Remember

If you're prone to anaphylactic reactions have an adrenaline pen close by.

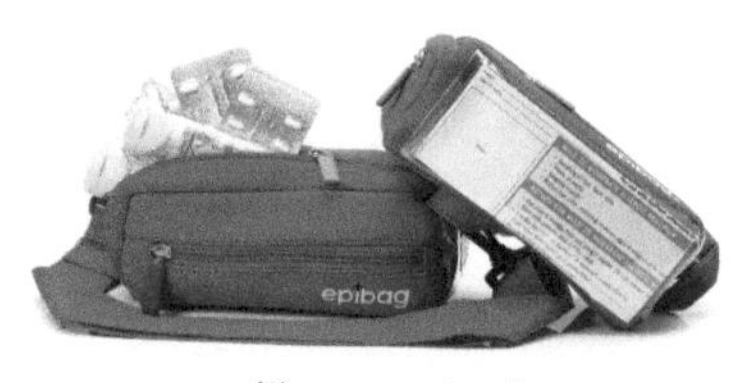
epibag
www.medibagaustralia.com

Pack your own safe food for when you are out and about.

If there isn't an adrenaline pen close by — *no food!*

Medicalert bracelets, bands and cards help warn others in an emergency.

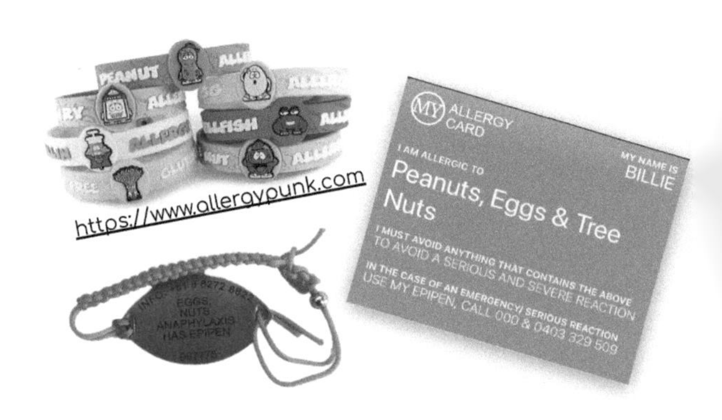
PEANUT
MY ALLERGY CARD
MY NAME IS BILLIE
I AM ALLERGIC TO
Peanuts, Eggs & Tree Nuts
I MUST AVOID ANYTHING THAT CONTAINS THE ABOVE TO AVOID A SERIOUS AND SEVERE REACTION
IN THE CASE OF AN EMERGENCY/ SERIOUS REACTION USE MY EPIPEN, CALL 000 & 0403 329 509
EGGS NUTS ANAPHYLAXIS HAS EPIPEN
https://www.allergypunk.com

Make sure to tell people about the role peanuts play in your day.

Ok Pete, time to say bye for now.

CPSIA information can be obtained
at www.ICGtesting.com
Printed in the USA
LVHW071309210422
716844LV00011B/318

* 9 7 8 1 9 2 2 5 9 3 0 0 9 *